J.B. Priestley

SUTTON POCKET BIOGRAPHIES

Series Editor C.S. Nicholls

Highly readable brief lives of those who have played a significant part in history, and whose contributions still influence contemporary culture.

SUTTON POCKET BIOGRAPHIES

J.B. Priestley

Dulcie Gray

Sutton Publishing

First published in 2000 by
Sutton Publishing Limited · Phoenix Mill
Thrupp · Stroud · Gloucestershire · GL5 2BU

British Library Cataloguing in Publication Data
A catalogue record for this book is available from the British
Library

ISBN 0-7509-1793-8

Typeset in 13/19pt Perpetua.
Typesetting and origination by
Sutton Publishing Limited.
Printed in Great Britain by
Cox & Wyman, Reading, Berkshire.

For Michael

CONTENTS

	Chronology	ix
	Family Tree	xiii
	Preface	xv
1	The Bradford Years	1
2	War – Marriage – Tragedy	12
3	Full-time Writer – Second Marriage	25
4	Jolly Jack	37
5	The Dramatist	46
6	Jane, Infidelity and Jacquetta	59
7	Postscripts – Family – Travelling	70
8	The 1970s and 1980s	81
	Notes	85
	Bibliography	87
	Priestley's Works	88

CHRONOLOGY

(Not all Priestley's publications are listed)

1894	**13 September.** J.B. Priestley born in Bradford
1896	Death of mother
1910	Leaves school
1914–18	First World War – serves on the front line in France with the Duke of Wellington's West Riding Regiment
1919	Demobilised. Enters Trinity Hall, Cambridge
1921	Marries Pat Tempest. Moves to London
1922	First book published: *Brief Diversions*
1923	Birth of first child, Barbara
1924	Birth of second child, Sylvia
1925	**25 November.** Death of wife Pat from cancer

Birth of Mary, Priestley's daughter by Jane Wyndham Lewis |
| **1926** | Marries Jane Wyndham Lewis and moves to Church Hanborough, Oxfordshire

George Meredith published |
| **1927** | *Adam in Moonshine* (novel) published |
| **1928** | *Benighted* (novel) |

Chronology

1929	*The Good Companions*
1930	Birth of daughter, Rachel
	Angel Pavement (novel)
1931	Has 'affair' with Peggy Ashcroft, actress
1932	Birth of son, Tom
	First West End play, *Dangerous Corner*
1933	Buys Billingham Manor and estate, Isle of Wight
1934	*English Journey* (travel)
1937	Three Priestley plays open: *Time and the Conways, I Have Been Here Before*, and *Music at Night*
	Midnight on the Desert
1938	*When We Are Married* (play)
1939	*Johnson Over Jordan* (play)
	Let the People Sing (novel)
1940	**June–October.** Broadcasts 'Postcripts' on BBC radio
1943	*Three Men in New Suits* (novel)
1946	*Bright Day*
1947	*An Inspector Calls* (play)
1948	*The Linden Tree* (play)
1949	*Delight* (essays)
1952	Divorced from Jane
	Dragon's Mouth (play)
1953	Marries Jacquetta Hawkes
1957	Initiates Campaign for Nuclear Disarmament
1960	*Literature and Western Man*
1962	*Margin Released* (memoirs)

Chronology

1965	*Lost Empires* (novel)
1968/9	*The Image Men* (novel, 2 vols)
1969–72	Historical trilogy: *The Prince of Pleasure* (1969), *The Edwardians* (1970), *Victoria's Heyday* (1972)
1975	*Particular Pleasures* (essays)
1977	Admitted to Order of Merit (OM)
1984	**14 August.** Death at his home, Kissing Tree House, near Stratford-upon-Avon

F A M I L Y   T R E E

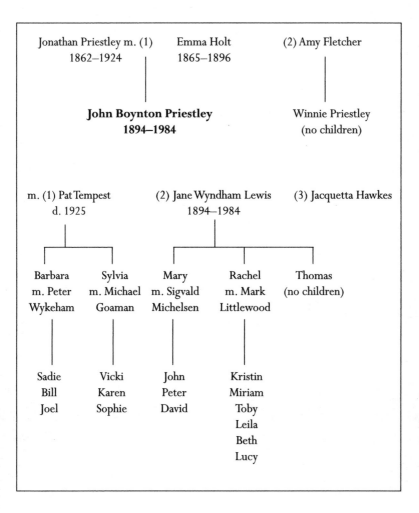

Jonathan Priestley m. (1) Emma Holt (2) Amy Fletcher
1862–1924   1865–1896

John Boynton Priestley Winnie Priestley
1894–1984   (no children)

m. (1) Pat Tempest (2) Jane Wyndham Lewis (3) Jacquetta Hawkes
d. 1925   1894–1984

Barbara	Sylvia	Mary	Rachel	Thomas
m. Peter	m. Michael	m. Sigvald	m. Mark	(no children)
Wykeham	Goaman	Michelsen	Littlewood	

Sadie	Vicki	John	Kristin
Bill	Karen	Peter	Miriam
Joel	Sophie	David	Toby
			Leila
			Beth
			Lucy

P R E F A C E

Dubbed ironically 'Jolly Jack' by those who did not
know him except in his sombre Yorkshire persona,
John Boynton Priestley could be jolly indeed. Light
on his feet both physically and in conversation, he
had many of the attributes of Falstaff – gusto,
patriotism, a delight in good living, and in spite of a
face like 'a glowering pudding' (his description),
considerable success with other men's wives.

There was of course much more to him. He was
a man of staggering versatility – outstandingly
successful as essayist, novelist, playwright,
autobiographer, critic, journalist (one article of his
in the *New Statesman* magazine triggered the
Campaign for Nuclear Disarmament) and
broadcaster (his famous 'Postscripts' during Battle
of Britain year were thought to have aroused the
jealousy of Winston Churchill). Emotionally a man
of the Left, and suspected by many of being a
communist fellow traveller, he disliked all

totalitarian systems. He never joined Labour or any other party and was in fact uneasy with all large organisations, including the Church, though there is a strong spiritual content to be found in his work. He never collected his First World War medals, refused all political honours but felt great satisfaction when awarded the OM by the Queen.

He was the despair of those who wished 'for his own good' – or for theirs – to pigeonhole him. Expecting another *Good Companions* after its enormous success they got *Angel Pavement* – an introverted story of the demise of a small business in a London cul-de-sac. Grumbling or jolly, JBP was 'as English as Steak & Kidney pudding' in his own words; an outstanding contributor both to 'Literature and Western Man' – incidentally the title of one of his most rewarding works, a book which once begun is impossible to put down.

I must declare an interest here. My husband, Michael Denison, and I loved him, and with good reason. He gave Michael his first important professional part in a West End revival of *Dangerous Corner*; a showy part as a Communist poet in *Music at Night* – his last before the Army claimed him –

and his first on his return six years later in *Ever Since Paradise*. Finally, in *Dragon's Mouth*, a first collaboration with his third wife, Jacquetta Hawkes, he gave us both two of the best roles in our long and varied careers. Add nearly fifty years of friendship, and civilised hospitality (though he could be an awkward guest!), our debt to him is clear.

The author and publisher gratefully acknowledge the permission of the Estate of J.B. Priestley to quote from *Rain Upon Godshill* by J.B. Priestley, on pages 47–8.

THE BRADFORD YEARS

The child born to Jonathan and Emma Priestley at 34 Mannheim Road, Toller Lane, Bradford, on 13 September 1894 was christened simply John, a name which, certainly in adult life, nobody ever called him. He was always known as Jack. Boynton came later and was his own invention, possibly to add rhythm and gravitas when he became an aspiring author – JBP perhaps sounding more important than JP. (Boynton is a village in the East Riding that he visited once or twice, so perhaps that gave him the idea.)

Jonathan Priestley, his father, was the son of an illiterate mill worker who somehow scraped enough money together to send him to a Teacher Training College, an opportunity of which the young man took full advantage, becoming an excellent schoolmaster with the vital ability to instil both knowledge and discipline in his flock. He was also a pillar of the Baptist chapel, and in JBP's words 'the man socialists have in mind when they write about socialism'.[1]

Little is known of Emma Priestley, née Holt, who died of ovarian cancer at the age of thirty-one, two years after her son was born, leaving him to the care of a grandmother, whom he adored, and who, when his parents were out for the evening, gave him rice pudding and told him stories of the West Riding in the 1840s and 1850s – 'Ten university lecturers and twenty certified teachers could not have given me as much as she did . . . illuminating everything, was the magic that begins with personal experience . . . close to wonder'.[2] In due course Jonathan's second wife, Amy Fletcher, was a loving stepmother to the little boy – 'kind and affectionate' was Priestley's own description of her.

Emma, probably a mill girl, was a typically jolly member of that put-upon breed and was once turned out of a theatre for laughing in the wrong place. But this was hearsay – her son had no recollection of her at all, although very occasionally he referred to her in rather romantic terms and described her as witty. Another story about her was that when she became bored with an overlong meeting of educationalists taking place in her front parlour, she fixed a hat on a broom handle and paraded outside the window to persuade them to finish. She had two brothers, one of whom, Tom, was said to have worked in the music halls – was this perhaps an inspiration for Priestley's book *Lost Empires* written in 1965? Tom became one of the best-known publicans in Bradford at the Volunteer Hotel in Green Lane.

In 1903 came a half-sister for John, and the family moved to a larger house further up Toller Lane at 5 Saltburn Place. This was the real home of childhood and adolescence, the home of memories, of sharing his father's passion for walking in the Dales, but of being unable to follow his rigid Baptist beliefs and worship on Sundays. It was here he encountered a female dragon of a schoolmistress at the school to and from which he walked every day. This woman terrified him and made education a nightmare. Fortunately, before it was too late, there came into his life one of those inspired teachers who open windows on to unsuspected landscapes. His name was Richard Pendlebury and the adult Priestley never forgot his enthusiasm for the spoken and written word, which he communicated to his eager pupil at Belle Vue High School, Bradford. For Priestley now had a room of his own – an attic – at Saltburn Place and in it he was beginning to write whenever opportunity offered.

Opportunity was soon to be limited to the lamplit hours because, as might be expected, when Priestley confronted his father with a request that he should leave school early, the latter, who had hopes of the boy winning the University Scholarship, which was well within his capabilities, was dismayed. But not for long. The 'work ethic' was strong in Jonathan Priestley. 'Then you must get a job,' he said; and though his socialism made him no friend to the iniquities of the wool trade (particularly the practice of sending small children to school in the morning and to the mills in the afternoon), there was little else for an unqualified adolescent to do in Bradford. And so at the age of fifteen Priestley became a very junior clerk at Helm & Co.

His duties were making copies of letters and running errands for the boss, a formidable figure with one saving grace – a passion for books. So the junior clerk would frequently find himself in the congenial atmosphere of the lending library where he could 'fleet the time carelessly' after finding the Boss's requirements.

Was the Boss aware of this, and perhaps even sympathetic out of thwarted literary ambitions of his own when young? There were certainly ample opportunities to sack the young man which were passed over – for instance, as Priestley wrote in *Margin Released* (1962) fifty years later: 'On several mornings, when the sun was already climbing high and there was not a cloud, I turned my back on the tram to town and went striding the opposite way, playing truant, to walk all day across the moors . . . I was, I remember, never happier; my mind was no more overshadowed with guilt than the sky was with cloud; the thought that here I was, alone and free, while others of my kind were at their desks, added brightness and gold to the sunlight, freshness to the air, music to the singing larks . . . Every moment of those truant walks is alive in me still;

perhaps I would not be writing now, if it were not for them.'[3]

Priestley's surplus energies, and they were many, were concentrated on exotic variations of wardrobe – there was a bright green suit worn with a floppy tie and a broad-brimmed hat which must have caused a sensation among Bradford's universal subfusc. These he might have worn at the theatre perhaps, to win the heart of one of his two simultaneous inamoratas: Miss Mabel Sealby, then Principal Girl of the Theatre Royal pantomime, or the other – more accessible if prosaic – the girl next door? Nothing, beyond the familiar agonies and ecstasies of unrequited adolescent love, came of either.

The obsessive writer was also all his life a voracious reader – the fruit of which would emerge in 1960 in that marvellous book *Literature and Western Man*. All this activity took place in his attic, the importance of which can be gauged by his borrowing the description of it from his favourite novel *Bright Day* (1946) almost word for word for the autobiographical *Margin Released* (1962) which came sixteen years later. The makeshift bookcases made of orange boxes, their contents bought at twopence a volume out of his eightpence lunch money; and the gas fire, 'a fierce little thing which couldn't begin to warm the room without grilling your shins', are common to both, and in *Bright Day* he adds 'two angry little gas mantles, white and trembling with fury'.[4] Two dilapidated armchairs meant that he could entertain a friend – but no girls were allowed by the strict disciplinarian downstairs.

Strangely, *Bright Day*'s 'hazy glimpse of the Moorland Skyline' has not survived into *Margin Released*; but by then the view from his window was of The Needles, though he remained emotionally attached to his native landscape all his days. The narrator of *Bright Day* sums up for both of them: 'I doubt if any room I have occupied since – although I have ranged at some expense from Amalfi to Santa Barbara, California – has ever brought me such a satisfying sense of possession as that one did.'[5]

Priestley's literary output – prose, verse, articles for the local press – was typed for him by a 'saucy dark lass who was paid in kisses', there being no cash available. 'Magic' is a frequently recurring word in Priestley's work, and the search for it and the desire to communicate it was a *leitmotif* of the man's creativity. The search began early, and there was even a mysterious mound in a field frequented by the four-year-old who was convinced it contained some magical treasure. As he grew older the most practical and accessible source of magic was in Bradford's theatres; and Priestley's delight as a member of the audience would eventually be transformed into a desire to be a purveyor of magic as a playwright.

Magic of another sort had meanwhile come his way in the shape of Esther, a friendly and available girl three years his senior who introduced him to sex. Grateful though he was, he never fell in love with her – she was too companionable and cosy to give birth to a grand passion on his part. Beer-assisted sing-songs with his mates – his own voice being the loudest, if not the most musical – were another source of delight. The adult Priestley cared deeply for serious music and incorporated it into a number of his plays.

The most unexpected source of magic in his life was a by-product of his employment at Helm & Co.

The firm's trade was largely the export of wool to romantic foreign destinations – Indian and Chinese addresses fired the junior clerk's imagination as he laboriously copied them out. There were also the free passages offered by a shipping line to wool trade employees, of which he took full advantage. His first trip was to Copenhagen, which he found dazzlingly bright and clean compared with Bradford. And the girls! Blonde and rosy-cheeked; what a contrast with their pale sisters living under the smoky skies of the West Riding. The next summer a walking tour of the Rhine Valley reinforced his love of travel, and a final visit to Amsterdam opened his eyes to Vermeer, Rembrandt and Van Gogh.

Rejection slips suddenly gave way in 1913 to a most unlikely job – a side effect of which began to reconcile Jonathan Priestley to the reality of his son's literary ambitions. The local Labour Party, of which young Priestley was not a member (though his father presumably was), engaged him to write a feature called 'Round the Hearth' which appeared over the initials JBP – the first time they had appeared in print, although he was not actually paid. He was amazed that a serious political journal should have given the freedom of its pages to an eighteen-year-old non-member of the party. But freedom it certainly was to range wider still and wider into theatrical criticism (including advocacy of a municipal theatre if major stars were to be encouraged to visit Bradford more frequently), and even to comments on the darkening international scene. Perhaps this proved too much for the editor of the *Bradford Pioneer*, for 'Round the Hearth' was discontinued. JBP was not discouraged. His ambition to become a writer burned even more brightly.

London Opinion, a popular national weekly, eventually bought a story of his – 'Secrets of the Rag Time King' – which described the amazing invasion of Bradford by American jazz. He received a guinea in recompense but much more in terms of satisfaction, and a further thaw in his father's attitude.

The rest of the family were on holiday, and Priestley was at home when he learned that Britain was at war with Germany. The *Bradford Pioneer*'s roving correspondent should not have been surprised, but he had seen nothing of military preparations in his idyllic trips to Germany, and so, in spite of much anti-German material in the press, he felt no sudden burst of patriotic fervour. He felt rather, and understandably, that this latest folly of the politicians was going to put paid indefinitely to a literary career which seemed on the point of take-off. In September 1914 he joined the Duke of Wellington's West Riding Regiment (the Dirty Duke's) in Halifax.

WAR – MARRIAGE – TRAGEDY

Priestley's motives for such an early enlistment were a mystery to himself, though he knew what they weren't. When he could bring himself to write about it many years later in *Margin Released* he would describe it as 'almost like a conscription of the spirit, little to do really with King and Country and flag-waving and hip-hip-hurrah, a challenge to what we felt was our untested manhood'.[1] Army life brought Priestley into contact with the officer class – a new phenomenon to him with its speech patterns, dress code, arrogance and privileges. These last he might have accepted if they had been allied to patent skills in the art of war, but too often the officers appeared mere amateurs, whose orders were nevertheless a matter of life and death. Many were as young as he; and the senior ones were no better, maintaining peace-time rituals in their châteaux – worse even, because of their capacity to send ever larger numbers of men to their deaths. As he told Diana Collins (later with her husband, Canon Collins, one of his greatest friends), he spent the first year trying to be a hero, and the rest of the time trying to stay alive.

Priestley found himself, a born civilian, deeply divided between the wasteful horror and the comedy of military life. The war left on him a scar which gave him depressions which plagued him for the rest of his life, just as walking on the Yorkshire moors had given him the capacity for joy.

In due course the regiment was moved to Surrey under canvas, eleven men to a tent; their uniforms were removed – more urgently needed elsewhere – and they were clad in blue dungarees and forage caps from which the dye spread over their faces when they were inspected in pouring rain by, of all people, Lord Kitchener, whose image was familiar to all from the famous poster 'Your Country Needs You'. 'The image I retained was of a rather bloated purplish face . . . of some larger-than-life yet now less-than-life figure,' said

Priestley. '. . . Yet it was he – and he alone – who
had raised us new soldiers out of the ground. This
. . . was a stroke of genius . . . I was, I still am, on
his side.'[2]

From their tents they moved gratefully to brick
barracks in Aldershot and then were marched the
hundred miles to Folkestone, something which to
his surprise Priestley greatly enjoyed (he was a
marathon walker after all). Was this to be their point
of departure for France? No, they were inexplicably
moved to Maidstone. Priestley progressed from
Lance Corporal to Company Billeting Officer,
which gave him pleasurable opportunities to chat up
potential landladies, to Battalion Post Corporal
which involved him in continuous and boring
enquiries about missing mail. At last his regiment
embarked for France. A long, blisteringly hot and
dusty march brought them to the line where they
were to relieve a regular division. In this area the
two front lines were wide apart, but this meant that
'listening posts' had to be established at night in No
Man's Land. On his second night at the front Lance
Corporal Priestley was two or three hours alone in
one of these, 'staring so hard at black nothing that it

stopped being black or nothing and began to crawl with greyish shapes . . . I do not think I am flattering my twenty-year-old self if I say that I was less apprehensive in that listening post than I am now on all manner of comparatively safe occasions. Youth, hard training, a genuine desire to get *into* the war at some point, had turned me temporarily into a brave soldier. I was less and less brave, in that sense, the more and more I saw of this war.'[3] The noise of the artillery and, even worse, the sodden squalor of the living conditions, he found more wearing (particularly after a spell out of the line) than the dangers to which they returned.

Priestley was wounded by a grenade splinter in the hand which involved a spell in hospital and convalescence at Le Treport. The latter he heartily disliked; they were underfed, cut off from their mates and mail from home, and subjected to continuous fatigues. Soon after his return to the front the whole division was moved to take over a sinister position from the French. Here they were welcomed by a great naval gun and more effectively by the *Minenwerfer* (mortars), which, being short-range, gave you less time to escape. Priestley was distributing the rations one morning in June 1916 – not a regular duty but one which on this occasion may have saved his life. He was in a small dug-out and the mortar shell landed in the trench just outside. Shortly afterwards he was severely wounded and sent home with gas gangrene.

There now began a protracted period of convalescence in stately homes with ravishing 'county' VAD girls whose songs and violin solos he would accompany in his rough and ready style on the piano, or in a camp near Ripon where all was mud, petty restrictions, and barrel-chested PT instructors who had never heard a shot fired in anger. A way of escape must be found and he decided belatedly to apply for a commission. Training in North Wales followed; he was then posted to the Devon Regiment's HQ at Devonport. There he remained for months, not being summoned to return to France until summer 1918. A few days after joining his new battalion he was gassed. Although he had his mask on in a flash, a trace of gas must have leaked in. He celebrated his escape with a generous intake of rum; and when the Germans attacked the next morning in a thick mist he was soon lost and wandered aimlessly, his head swimming with a cocktail of gas and rum, trying to find the battle. Eventually he fell asleep in a welcoming shell-hole where he was discovered by two stretcher-bearers. Thus ended his last experience of action in the war.

Unfit for active service, he was posted to Rouen where his duties included casting comedians needed by unit concert parties. Suddenly the war was over, and this ghostly collection of all ranks in Rouen hung about trying to get suitably drunk. Next, ironically, came what he regarded as his most important assignment in the war – protecting the interests of 600 German prisoners and their British guards. It was to involve him in a head-on clash with the top brass of Army HQ. He had been ordered to move his prisoners to a site which, on inspection, he found to be entirely unsuitable for men, both German and English, who were far from fit. HQ told him to get on with it. He refused, provoking a descent of military police threatening a court martial. He was able to tell them that nearby he had found a ruined German hutted camp and that if HQ would leave him alone, he undertook that his Germans would build their own huts on the site at no expense to anyone. Consent was grudgingly given, the camp rose, and, even better, in March 1919 he was told he could go home.

In 1919, clad in an ill-fitting 'demob' suit (his clothes, except on special occasions, continued to have a flavour of demob), he emerged into the unfamiliar light of civilian life eager to put the war behind him. He had no detailed long-term plan – he never had all his life. (He was always so full of ideas that it was a question of waiting until one came insistently to the surface, and then there would be total commitment.) In 1919 his 'plans' were an amalgam of rediscovering the Dales and writing articles and essays aimed at the multitude of periodicals that were then such a feature of the literary scene. There was nothing there to make the prospect of marriage and raising a family a practical possibility, but this was very much on his mind. There was a girl, Pat Tempest, who worked in the Bradford library, where they had met and where the relationship developed to the extent that she wrote to him regularly during the war, and visited him in hospital after he was wounded. She also typed for him, and he accompanied her violin solos on the piano. Photographs show her as attractive, though fine-drawn.

An ex-serviceman's grant then offered Priestley a place at Trinity Hall, Cambridge, to read English and history. He did not take to Cambridge, nor Cambridge to him. He hated the flat Fen Country, quite unrewarding for walking compared with the moors, and the dons and undergraduates spoke with accents quite different from his. His years in Flanders made the whole institution of the university seem divorced from reality. However, it gave him food and shelter and the opportunity to assuage his hunger for the written word, thus forming an important early foundation for *Literature and Western Man*.

He made some friends, notably a poet, Edward Davison, who opened to him the pages of the *Cambridge Review*, of which he was editor. But Priestley always felt a refugee from Yorkshire, uneasy with the rituals of dinner, High Table and those 'private income accents'. In spite of taking his degree in two years, rather than the ususal three, he got respectable second-class degrees in his chosen subjects (he had switched to history and political science), which decided him to use the remainder of the grant given for this to return for a postgraduate year. He would rent a house and somehow manage to bring Pat down as his bride. This daring plan was a success. They were married on 29 June 1921 at the Westgate Chapel in Bradford with as little fuss as possible, the bridegroom describing the occasion as 'one of those plunges into married life preceded by total ignorance of the person involved'.

Money was desperately short in spite of all Priestley's efforts at coaching, reviewing and writing essays for the *Cambridge Review*. He decided to find a local publisher who might bring out a collection of these to be entitled *Brief Diversions* (1922). It was a slim volume of sixty pages, and although – or perhaps because? – it satirised such luminaries as Sir Arthur Quiller-Couch (then Professor of English), Alfred Noyes the poet, and W.B. Yeats, the Irish man of letters, it received rave reviews, and won him the enthusiastic patronage of J.C. Squire at the influential *London Mercury*, and the offer of reviews by Robert Lynd at the *Daily News*. What it did not produce was royalties. Pat, by now pregnant, understandably wanted the security of a steady job from him – such as the offer of a lectureship in north Devon. But he turned it down; the urge to concentrate on writing was too strong. He even compounded his rashness by deciding to quit the shelter of Cambridge where Quiller-Couch, in spite of *Brief Diversions*, had offered him some lectures on English literature, and with a capital of £50 and a wife whose pregnancy was proving difficult, he went to London as a freelance writer.

Barbara, the first child, was born in March 1923 and soon Pat was pregnant again with Sylvia, an even more difficult birth (on 30 April 1924), which was followed by the discovery at Guy's Hospital of a fatal bladder cancer. For the sake of Pat and the children the Priestleys decided to move out of the flat they had been sharing with Edward Davison, and went to Chinnor Hill in the Buckinghamshire countryside. But Pat's health did not respond as hoped, and longer and longer visits to Guy's Hospital were needed.

It was against this tragic background that Priestley's career began to take off. Squire and Lynd were as good as their word; he became a reader for the Bodley Head (and was proud of having recommended the first novels of Graham Greene and C.S. Forester) and Methuen's requested a sight of all his unpublished works. Attendance at literary parties, even though as he once told me he hated the 'yookety-yack of stand-up dos', became a time-consuming obligation, if he was to make the most of his growing reputation. At one of these there was a chance encounter with a Mrs Jane Wyndham Lewis which was to dominate the domestic background of his life for a quarter of a century. Jane, whose marriage was in difficulties, clearly felt that the meeting was significant for she confessed to a fellow guest, 'That is an extraordinary man – I am going to marry him.'

Life for him now was complicated and stressful in the extreme. He was commuting from Chinnor daily, where Pat's mother was looking after the two little girls, and paying agonising visits to Pat in hospital. There was also a growing mutual attraction between him and Jane Wyndham Lewis, and the varied but always urgent demands of his literary activities. He got back to Chinnor one evening so overcome with despair that he was nearly out of his mind. Chinnor was utterly remote, with no pub, no cinema, nothing to take his mind off things for a couple of hours. 'I decided to write something – anything – a few pages to be torn up after I felt less wretched. On my desk was a rough list of chapters for the [projected] Meredith book. I chose one of the chapters, not the first, and slowly, painfully set to work on it. In an hour I was writing freely and well. It is in fact one of the best chapters in the book. And I wrote myself out of my misery, followed a trail of thought and words into daylight.'[4] The poet and novelist, George Meredith (1829–1909), best known for *Poems and Lyrics of the Joy of Earth* and *Diana of the Crossways* (his most popular novel), was a contributor to many periodicals. He wrote continuously for fifty years. He also sat for Henry Wallis's painting, *The Death of Chatterton*; his wife, Mary Ellen Nicholls, later left him for Wallis.

The daylight would be short-lived. By now (1924) he and Jane had become lovers and when she belatedly discovered he was married and she was pregnant she disappeared into the blue. In June he lost his much loved and respected father. He moved back into London; Pat was able briefly to be with him, but the inexorable spread of the cancer forced her back into hospital; in March 1925 Jane gave birth to a daughter, Mary, christened as Wyndham Lewis but soon known as Priestley. There is evidence that the dying Pat was aware of Jane's existence, but her chief concern, as demonstrated in letters to her mother, was for the financial burden her illness was causing Jack. 'As a matter of fact, it is not as easy to die as one might think,' she wrote.[5] In the autumn of 1925 her brave fight ended. She had been the love of his youth. With her death and that of his father, his own youth was buried.

THREE

FULL-TIME WRITER – SECOND MARRIAGE

Considering his experiences on the domestic front during the twenties, Priestley's literary and journalistic output both before and after his bereavement was astonishing. True, it needed to be if he were to keep abreast of the expenses of Pat's illness; but his motivation was not restricted to that tragic circumstance. It was and would always be the essence of the man himself, as it had been of the boy in the attic; and the only breaks in the output were during the Second World War and in old age when, apart from natural exhaustion, he felt the world was out of joint and would not listen to him any more.

After the *succès d'estime* of *Brief Diversions* in 1922, there was a return in *Figures in Modern Literature*

(1924) to the style of acute but basically friendly observation of distinguished personalities. This time he sent presentation copies to all his subjects. One of them, George Santayana, whom he described as 'a philosophical and literary League of Nations', said he admired the courage with which in criticising people who were still living, Priestley had faced the hard choice between truth and courtesy, and courtesy had carried the day.

This was more criticism than praise. 'You do not reach the centre,' Santayana said. Arnold Bennett and A.E. Housman answered on similar though highly individual lines. Greatly daring, Priestley sent a copy of a more serious work, *George Meredith* (1926, edited by J.C. Squire and published by Macmillan), to Thomas Hardy, and received solid praise from the great man.

It may be fanciful to suggest that the contrast in the weight of criticism had a profound effect on Priestley and led him away from witty but facile criticism towards the deeper waters of creative writing.

Between *Meredith* and the end of the decade there were four – largely reprinted – books of essays and also four novels: *Adam in Moonshine* (1927), *Benighted* (1927), *Farthing Hall* (1929) in collaboration with Hugh Walpole) and *The Good Companions* (1929). There was also a biography of Thomas Love Peacock (1927).

Though Pat's death removed a financial burden from Priestley's life there was nothing simple about the future that faced him. Pat had left two small daughters, Sylvia and Barbara; Jane Wyndham Lewis had given him a third, Mary. Priestley had hesitations about marrying again. Was the fierce mutual attraction between him and Jane an appropriate basis for marriage and the bringing up of four children? For Angela, too, Jane's child by her first husband, the writer Wyndham Lewis, must not be forgotten. Jane also had her misgivings. She had just successfully sued her husband for divorce on the grounds of adultery.

The needs of the children won and on 26 September 1926 Priestley and Jane were married. Jack and his daughters moved into Jane's home. College House, a large and attractive house and garden at Church Hanborough in Oxfordshire, could comfortably accommodate a household of six and a nanny, and even provided a detached space in the loft of the former dairy where Priestley could write, secure from the patter of tiny feet. Priestley was in fact a devoted father and, provided the children scrupulously observed the house rules which required – from Jane as well – total non-interference when he was working, he would emerge in the jolliest mood prepared to play games both childish and imaginative until his small audience was happily exhausted. Of course the mood was not always jolly and then the whole household would go in fear of an explosion or, even worse, a lowering silence.

Jane, a volatile character who lived on her nerves, presented problems to them all. Of medium height, with dark hair and a Welsh lilt to her musical voice, she took a degree in French and Italian, and later learned to read Russian and Portuguese but never pursued any academic career, her creative energy being absorbed by the homes she created. That she was rarely relaxed in her marriage is perhaps explained by the speed with which Priestley embarked on a string of infidelities –

some trivial, at least two matrimonially shattering. But however tragic, confusing and blissful these might be, they would never be allowed to interfere with his *raison d'être* — to be a writer. When Pat was dying in 1925 he was engaged among much else with *The English Comic Characters* (1925), a book much loved by the theatrical profession; and during the first four years of his marriage to Jane came four novels.

After the enormous success of *The Good Companions* and *Angel Pavement* (1930) Heinemann, now his publishers, decided to republish *Adam in Moonshine* and *Benighted* with a new preface by Priestley. This is a core document which shows his attitude to the writing of fiction:

Where I differ from most is my conviction that the novel demands some sort of objective narrative . . . a story, and if possible, a fairly shapely one, no matter how strong [the writer's] subjective interests may be. Indeed, I consider this . . . easily the most difficult problem a modern novelist is called upon to face . . . I thought I saw a possible solution in some form of dramatic symbolism, in narrative that would move, so to speak, in two worlds at once.

These words were written after the four novels were completed. But what evidence is there in them that the narrative 'moving in two worlds at once' was already at work? Quite a lot, though it had not, of course, reached the assurance of later works. *Adam in Moonshine* was a romp about a young man caught up in a series of adventures on the Yorkshire moors – a plain tale indeed except that the people he meets fade out of his life at the conclusion of each adventure so completely that the reader is left wondering whether they really existed at all or whether they were no more than part of 'the vague and changing pageant' of his ideas.

Benighted, which followed, was a richer and more complex illustration of Priestley's theories. The setting is the classic remote and sinister house; the travellers who seek shelter there on a night of appalling weather are ordinary folk; not so the inmates they encounter when the great door is opened to them. The Femms and their hulking mute servant are straight out of Gothic melodrama, and the reader cannot help feeling that the author enjoyed laying it on thick. The heart of the story occurs when the shell-shocked young Penderel, reliving the ever present threat of obliteration in the trenches as he dozes in front of the fire, is suddenly aware that the Frankenstein-like figure of Saul the mad servant is moving towards him down the stairs – a dramatic symbol perhaps of war itself. Bravely Penderel faces the monster and hears it shuffling away. He knows a moment of inexpressible euphoria. He has banished war for ever, by a show of courage. The shadow of death is lifted and he can look forward to a shining future. The vision is to be short-lived and Saul returns; there is a fierce struggle on the stairs and both die.

Benighted is no masterwork. The boundaries between the melodramatic narrative and the deeply felt evocation of the war are perhaps too sharp. But both elements are highly effective, and the denouement, bringing together the death of war and of its victims, is indeed the end of a well-shaped tale.

Soon after Pat's death there began to ferment in Priestley's mind the idea of a long picaresque novel. When eventually he broached the idea to Heinemann, they did their utmost to dissuade him. Long novels were expensive to produce and hard to sell. Neither consideration weighed with Priestley, but the financial facts of life caused a postponement which might have turned into a cancellation but for the providential arrival in his life of Hugh Walpole.

Walpole, an immensely popular novelist of the 1920s and early 1930s, though never achieving his ambition to reach the literary peaks to which he aspired, was invited by letter from an unknown J.B. Priestley to contribute to a series called 'These Diversions' which Priestley was editing. Intrigued, Walpole invited him to his home in the Lake District. 'I find Priestley very agreeable,' he wrote in his diary. 'He is cocksure and determined but has a great sense of humour about himself.' And a few days later after the joys of fell-walking: 'Priestley is certainly a very clever man . . . he will . . . go far.'[1]

Inevitably, as the friendship developed, the subject of the picaresque novel came up, and the necessity for Priestley to set aside all other projects until it was achieved, and to be able to afford to do so. Walpole already had an enviable record of help to younger writers, T.S. Eliot, Graham Greene and Dylan Thomas being among his beneficiaries. But he realised that a straight loan would not be acceptable to the cocksure young Yorkshireman, so he devised a plan both practical and sensitive. He invited Priestley to collaborate with him on a book, knowing that his name on the cover would ensure a far bigger advance and royalties than Priestley could command on his own, and would give him the freedom from financial worry that was essential for such a major enterprise.

So *Farthing Hall* was born. It took the form of letters between two friends, a middle-aged scholar (Priestley) and a bright young man (Walpole, although he was ten years older than his collaborator). Priestley, explaining the unusual 'casting' later, said that Walpole's basically sunny disposition was more suited than his own to romantic youth. *Farthing Hall* suffered from its form, but it achieved what the generous Walpole intended and what Priestley so badly needed — he could commit himself to *The Good Companions*, the roots of which lay in the dark days that had preceded it — the four years of war, and Pat's illness and death. A holiday of the spirit was needed from such protracted darkness, and so he chose a fairy story.

Three disparate characters (Inigo Jollifant, a refugee from teaching at a terrible preparatory school; Jess Oakroyd, a robust man of all trades and dissatisfied with the lot, and Elizabeth Trant, a 'lady', who has been released from servitude by the death of her widowed father, and has bought herself a car and is in search of adventure) meet by chance in a tea-room of a Midland town. It is not large and they find they are sharing it with the Dinky-Doos, a concert party on the verge of collapse. They start talking and before they break up, the Dinky-Doos have become the Good Companions; Miss Trant will finance the venture, Inigo will compose new musical numbers, and Jess will build the sets. Unlikely perhaps, but unlikeliness is the very essence of the magic of fairy stories. What makes this one different, what gives it paradoxically its special magic, is the documentary reality of the background – the squalid theatrical digs, the cross-country railway journeys, the triumphs and disasters depending on the mood of their audiences, the fellowship, the jealousies, the whole theatrical scene in miniature. Against this setting Priestley sets his characters to work and play. The book also teems with notable minor characters, always one of Priestley's strong suits, and there is nothing finer than Jess Oakroyd's farewell to his shrewish wife on her deathbed when after several characteristic swipes at him for his shortcomings as husband and father she says quietly, 'I'm bad Jess.'

Priestley does not forget the uncertainty of all theatrical enterprises – he was writing long before the advent of the seemingly everlasting runs of our current mega-musicals. He sees clearly the effect on the individual Good Companions of such uncertainty, another feature which distances the book from the backstage sentimentality which many readers think of as its basic character. Nothing annoyed him more. 'Those bloody *Good Companions*,' he once said to me when I was praising *Lost Empires*, 'anyone would think I'd never written anything else!'

In spite of the enthusiasm of C.S. Evans, a Heinemann director to whom Priestley sent the first half of the book ('It has humour, humanity and exuberance, three of the very rarest qualities of our time,' came the reply),[2] the board thought that an initial run of 10,000 copies was the maximum risk they should take. Subdued sales in the summer seemed to support their judgement but with the approach of Christmas all was transformed. The weekly sales were soon running at 2,000 a week, reaching a peak over Christmas of 5,000 a day.

This overwhelming success made Priestley a national figure. It aroused the enthusiasm of the public which he enjoyed, and created the myth, which he did not, of the shrewd Yorkshireman giving readers exactly what they wanted for a pot of gold. 'A modest run of luck,' he wrote in *Margin Released* (1962), 'just beyond the limit of our expectations, would have done me much good and no possible harm. Not so this giant jackpot, this golden gusher, this genie out of the bottle.'

JOLLY JACK

Was the almost universal acceptance of the description of Jack Priestley as a dour, humourless north countryman forever smoking a pipe, due largely to his disgruntled reaction to the huge success of *The Good Companions?* The book was published at the time of the Great Depression, and fellow writers and critics showed their envy and their claws very clearly. Why, when most people were having a very difficult time, could he not rejoice in his good fortune? He became to them a sort of Quisling of letters who had committed the ultimate vulgarity of becoming a best-seller – one moreover translated into twenty-two languages.

The reality was very different. He was very often Jolly Jack, and a marvellous mimic, raconteur and companion, though he himself did not think so. In a letter to Hugh Walpole he wrote

'I can never understand that anybody should find pleasure in my company, and when they do I always think there's a catch in it.' He was inventively funny, and his small shouts of laughter, when he bared his teeth a little, and slightly shook his shoulders, and his kindness to anyone in trouble were endearing. As his widow Jacquetta Hawkes said to me after he died, 'He was strangely misunderstood. He was such a sweet fellow.'

There is an engaging story of him at one of the lavish weekend parties that Jane gave when they lived on the Isle of Wight. The poet Alfred Noyes was among the guests, with his small son, who was dressed to Jack's horror like Little Lord Fauntleroy. Jack glowered at the child throughout, and the little boy was crushed. On the Monday morning, any guests still at Brook Hill, the house where Priestley then lived, were treated to a visit to the bull on Jane's farm – and given a blow-by-blow description of his prowess at servicing the cows. Alfred Noyes was shocked. 'No, no, Jane!' he exclaimed, 'Not in front of the child, please! He is too young to know the facts of life.' 'Then don't tell him!' roared Jack, 'Don't tell him. They are too good for him.'

Later on, on the day Jane left Jack for good, Thane Parker, who had worked for Jack for many years, since the long-ago days of the Mask Theatre Company at the Westminster Theatre, came to Jack at his flat in Albany to tell him the news. Michael Denison and I were there having lunch. 'She has left you for a bird watcher,' he said. Jack seemed astounded by the news. 'A bird watcher? A bird watcher?' (Jane had in fact left Jack for the distinguished ornithologist, Dr David Bannerman, whom she later married.) 'Why should she do that? I've been a good husband.' As he was at the time indulging in two adulterous affairs, which were public knowledge, this seemed a strange point of view. Then his mood changed dramatically. 'Ring Mrs Hawkes,' he said to Thane, 'and invite her to Brook Hill for the weekend – and you'll come too, won't you?' he said, turning to us, 'I'll need your company as chaperones!' (He was also having an affair with Jacquetta Hawkes.) So we all went down to the Isle of Wight together, with Jacquetta's son Nicholas. On the way there all through the journey Jack kept saying, 'It will be all right, Jane's a lady. She won't have taken anything.' But she had.

Jack produced an enormous front door key, and led us into the house. The first room on the right was absolutely bare except for a pianola. The dining room had tables and chairs. The other rooms downstairs were stripped. Upstairs all was well, and Miss Pudduck, Jack's cook who looked after him until he died, and Gertrude the parlourmaid were still there (Gertrude later became Jack's housekeeper) and had made up the beds. Jack, having wandered around bemused, suddenly laughed – and we had a hilarious and wonderful few days with him, now in the sunniest of moods, mimicking, dancing, singing, and clowning.

Two other special occasions come to mind. A good friend of ours, Frankie Howerd, the comedian, had always wanted to meet Jack. In his book *Particular Pleasures* (1975) Jack had written a glowing piece on Howerd and his work, ending by saying, 'He (Frankie) is a very clever man pretending not to be'.[1] So Frankie asked me if I would ask him if they could meet. 'I'll ring him, and see if it can be arranged', I said. Jack was interested. 'I'd like that,' he said, 'but I'm not going up to bloody London to see him. Bring the lad here, you come too, and we'll have lunch.' 'Here' was Kissing Tree House, where he and Jacquetta had their home in Alveston, near Stratford-upon-Avon. Frankie was so nervous that when we reached Stratford a little early, I suggested that we should have a drink at the nearest pub. It was very crowded, and someone jogged Frankie's arm, sending the brandy and ginger ale he was drinking all down the front of his suit. Kind helpers tried to sponge it out with a wet cloth but he still looked rather odd as we arrived at Jack's.

Jack kissed me warmly, but seemed wary and a little formal with Frankie. We went up the marble-floored corridor to the large study with long windows facing the garden, and furnished from floor to ceiling with books, where Jack offered us drinks from the splendid bar concealed behind false bookshelves in the left-hand corner. Frankie asked for a brandy and ginger ale, and explained what had happened at the pub. Jack looked dour. 'I only have the best brandy,' he said, 'and I don't mix it with ginger ale.' He put two glasses in front of Frankie, and a bottle of brandy and one of ginger ale as well. This did nothing for Frankie's nerves – but he poured brandy into one glass, and ginger ale into the other, and sipped them anxiously in turn. Jack made no attempt to ease the situation and the going was difficult until lunch was announced, when suddenly the atmosphere lightened. Both men began to tell funny stories, and by the end of the meal they had become friendly, and Jacquetta and I had been royally entertained.

Priestley was a strange mixture of both good and bad moods. The dedication to *Delight* (1949) reads: 'For the Family – These Small Amends – with the Old Monster's Love'. He entitles the book's preface 'The Grumbler's Apology' and begins it:

> I have always been a grumbler. All the records going back to earliest childhood, establish this fact. Probably I arrived here a malcontent, convinced that I had been sent to the wrong planet. (And I feel even now there is something in this). I was designed for the part, for I have a sagging face, a weighty

underlip, what I am told is 'a saurian eye', and a rumbling but resonant voice from which it is difficult to escape. Money could not buy a better grumbling outfit.

Delight is a series of essays, and Priestley was lucky to be writing at a time when essays were popular, because he was one of the last of the great essayists. The second piece, called 'Shopping in Small Places', begins:

When I am in cities and surrounded by shops I take no pleasure in buying things and generally contrive to have my shopping done for me. Take me away from shops, however, and then after a week or two let me find my way to some small town or village and I take a delight in buying almost anything – I am as bad as any woman. I am like a sailor after a long voyage. I acquire gadgets and for a day or two have an almost painful loyalty toward them, the gadget and I being like an engaged couple and any criticism being instantly resented. Out of some general store I bring pencils I don't need, dubious scented tobacco, boiled sweets I have to give away, horrible stationery, travel books by Victorian clergymen, balls of string, patent medicines, hairy little note-books, boxes of paper fasteners. There is practically nothing I cannot be sold if I have been long enough away from shops.[2]

There was also a dark side to Priestley. He was a man with many devoted friends and in turn he was intensely loyal to them, but after a long friendship he turned away from Dame Rebecca West for good. Not knowing of this dislike we invited them both to our house and Jack refused to speak to Rebecca or even to look at her all the time they were with us. She was extremely distressed and said she had no idea why he was behaving in such a manner. He refused to say why, but announced passionately that he never wanted to be near her again. Rebecca told us later that the rift was never healed.

He was, however, kind to those in trouble. It was he who made our marriage in 1939 possible. Michael was under contract to him at the Mask Theatre, in his first London job. It was so badly paid that he hesitated to marry me. He was then offered another job at £9 a week. Jack gave him permission to break his contract and come with me to Aberdeen, provided he promised to go back to the

Westminster Theatre in September. This he did, soon after war was declared. The season opened with *Music at Night*, by Jack, and Michael played the excellent part of the communist poet. The London theatres had been closed when war was declared, and *Music at Night* was the first straight play to be put on.

FIVE

THE DRAMATIST

Priestley was one of the most prolific writers of the twentieth century. He wrote twenty-two books of fiction, fifty-two pieces of non-fiction, had thirty of his plays published, and thirty-nine performed. It is impossible therefore to write about them all in a work of this size. Iris Murdoch considered him a genius (he himself disagreed) and he was certainly a great man of letters. He professed no religion, though in *Music at Night* (1947) there is a God-like character to whom the others in the play chant 'All hail to the One Great Heart and Mind', and was in many ways a mystic – magic and a kind of awe were very much a part of his writing. The writing was full of variety, of ideas, and of a kind of search for how the world worked, from an almost metaphysical point of view. In the end he did find what he was looking for, in a strange dream he had, which had haunted him all his life:

I dreamt I was standing at the top of a very high tower, alone, looking down on millions of birds all flying in one direction, every kind of bird was there, all the birds in the world. It was a noble sight, this vast aerial river of birds. But now in some mysterious fashion the gear was changed and time speeded up, so that I saw generations of birds, and watched them break their shells, flutter into life, mate, weaken, falter and die. Wings grew only to crumble; bodies were sleek and then, in a flash, bled and shrivelled. And death struck everywhere at every second. What was the use of all this blind struggle towards life, this eager trying of wings, this hurried mating, this flight and surge, all this gigantic meaningless biological effort? As I stared down, seeming to see every creature's ignoble little history almost at a glance, I felt sick at heart. It would be better if not one of them, if not one of us all, had been born, if the struggle ceased forever. I stood on my tower, still alone, desperately unhappy. But now the gear was changed again and time went faster still, and it was rushing by at such a rate, that the birds could not show any movement, but were like an enormous plain sown with feathers. But along this plain, flickering through the bodies themselves, there now passed a sort of white flame, trembling, dancing, then hurrying on and as soon as I saw it I knew that this white flame was life itself, the very quintessence of being; and then it came to me, in a rocket-burst of ecstasy, that nothing mattered, nothing could ever matter, because nothing else was real but this quivering, hurrying lambency of being. Birds, men or creatures not yet shaped and coloured, all were of no account except so far as this flame of life travelled through them. It left nothing to mourn over behind it, what I had thought was tragedy was mere emptiness or a shadow show; for now all real feeling was caught and purified and danced on ecstatically with the white flame of life.[1]

The theatre was an immensely important part of Priestley's life – but, of his thirty-nine plays, only three have really lasted and are continually revived: *Dangerous Corner* (1932), *When We Are Married* (1938) and *An Inspector Calls* (1947). *Time and the Conways* (1937), *I Have Been Here Before* (1937) and *They Came to a City* (1943) are also occasionally performed.

Dangerous Corner (1932), Priestley's first play, was written in a week. It was in its way one of his 'Time' plays, foreshadowing *I Have Been Here Before* and *Time and the Conways*, and it was very ingenious. My husband Michael Denison played the part of Gordon in it, in the first of Priestley's Westminster

Theatre seasons. He made an instant success of the role, only months after he left drama school. However, the first showing of the play had a difficult time. The critics of the daily papers damned it, and the backers wanted to pull out, but Ivor Brown at the *Observer* and James Agate of the *Sunday Times* gave good notices. Priestley took the gamble of backing the play himself from the profits of *The Good Companions* and, after a few difficult days, the play took off and became a success. Priestley said he never really liked the play, 'for it seems to me to be merely an ingenious box of tricks'. On the other hand, it is excellent entertainment. Well written and crafted, it still appeals to audiences.

When We Are Married is a completely different kind of play, and very funny indeed. It was directed by Basil Dean and was an immediate success. Priestley had a love–hate relationship with it all his life. Three middle-aged very respectable north country couples meet to celebrate their silver wedding anniversaries. They had all been married on the same day by the same minister. The young 'lah-di-dah' organist who had played for them that day then tells them that they have never been married at all, as the minister who married them had not been licensed to do so. Despite the fact that soon after the play opened there came the Munich crisis and Chamberlain's promise of 'Peace in Our Time', it played to packed houses.

It opened in Manchester and eventually settled happily into the St Martin's Theatre in London. Frank Pettingell, who played the photographer, was suddenly taken ill. He had no understudy, and as no other actor could be found to take his place Priestley stepped into the part for twelve performances until Pettingell recovered. He found it very hard to learn his lines, although he himself had written them, and slept badly, very frightened that he would forget them on stage. He also found the end of every performance an anti-climax. However, he got rave reviews, and the publicity for his appearances stimulated the bookings at the box office even further.

An Inspector Calls, directed by Stephen Daldry, has run in London since 1993. It was written in the autumn of 1944 at great speed. Critics suggested that several London managements rejected it, but

Priestley said that it was the unavailability of a suitable theatre which made him send a copy of the script to Moscow in 1945. Ten weeks later two famous companies, the Leningrad Theatre Company and Tairov's Kamerny, were running it successfully simultaneously in Moscow. It then went on a European tour to several state theatres and finally came to the Old Vic in London, where it was given a cold reception. As it had run for 1,600 performances in Germany alone, Priestley was not unnaturally distressed.

The play, which owes a good deal to Ouspensky, concerns the Birling family who are celebrating an engagement party which is interrupted by the arrival of an Inspector who so skilfully and forcefully questions the family about the suicide of a girl called Eva Smith that they become frightened and uneasy. Eva Smith had been a strike leader at Birling's factory, and Birling had sacked her for asking for a weekly rise of half a crown. Birling's son has made her pregnant, and Miss Birling, his sister, has managed to get her dismissed from her next employment. The Inspector is challenged when his alleged photograph of Eva Smith is

suspected as a fake, but even when a telephone call
to the hospital reveals no trace of the dead girl, and
the local police station has never heard of the
Inspector, the family are still immersed in self-
justification. At last they see the Inspector as an
impostor, and become almost complacent about
their guilt – but the telephone suddenly rings to say
that the Inspector will call again because a girl who
has poisoned herself is now really dying in hospital.

Priestley loved the theatre for most of his life.
He also loved the actors he saw on their way to
the theatre in Bradford. He found them larger
than life in their trilby hats, with brilliantined
hair, their faces never quite free of the last
performance's make-up. The actresses seemed to
him to belong to a different and far superior
world from the other girls in Bradford. Priestley
himself wore large, felt, rather actory hats all his
life, and he somehow managed to make his
outdoor coats look like cloaks. He was always
sympathetic to actors, which made him an
excellent director. We worked with him on
Dragon's Mouth (1952), and I have seldom enjoyed
being directed more.

In the winter of 1937 Jack and Jane Priestley set off for Egypt, on a holiday that went wrong almost at once – but it had important results. During his time in the desert Priestley re-examined the philosophies of both J.W. Dunne, who wrote *An Experiment with Time*, and P.D. Ouspensky, and now for the first time he studied the works of Carl Jung. They fascinated and captivated him, and from them came the inspiration for his 'Time' plays, *I Have Been Here Before* and *Time and the Conways*. *Time and the Conways* is the better of the two, but both plays were put on simultaneously in two different London theatres, and they were based on two different theories of time. In *I Have Been Here Before* Dr Görtler, one of its main characters, believes that 'We move along a spiral track. It is not quite the same journey from the cradle to the grave each time – we must set out on the same road each time, but along that road we have a choice of adventures.'

Time and the Conways has no need to explain the theory of time – the play explains itself. Act I is set in 1919, Act II in 1937 and Act III in 1919. In Act I we meet the Conway family, setting off gaily for the mistakes and unhappiness which they will encounter. In Act II Kay says, 'Remember what we once were, and what we thought we'd be. And now this! And it's all we have. Alan it's us . . . the happy young Conways . . . they're gone, and gone forever.' Alan replies, 'They are real and existing – we're seeing another bit of the view – a bad bit if you like – but the whole landscape is still there.' Act III returns to when they are young.

Johnson over Jordan (1939) was Priestley's most ambitious and experimental play, with the starring role written for Ralph Richardson – at the time too young for the part, though he played it magnificently. It is a morality play about a man going into the after-life, and is the most advanced of the Time plays. Basil Dean again directed. Like many of Priestley's plays, it made great use of the music which Benjamin Britten wrote, and it needed a large orchestra, dancers and a very complicated lighting set-up. It is the day of Robert Johnson's funeral, and Johnson talks about his wife and what will happen to her on her own. He is existing in a kind of dream dimension. He is an ordinary man, only fifty-three years old, and he knows he is dead and must meet his destiny. He is finally alone on the stage, small and frightened – he shivers and turns up the collar of his coat – the brass blares, the drums beat, and Johnson, wearing his bowler hat and carrying his bag, slowly turns and walks towards a blue light and a constellation of stars.

The play opened at the New Theatre (London) in February 1939, then soon transferred to the Saville Theatre. It cost as much as a big musical, but did not attract a musical audience. The cheap seats were always filled, but not the stalls, and the play closed because it lost too much money.

On Priestley's seventy-fifth birthday the BBC compiled a television programme of celebration. Friends offered memories and loving portraits and there were readings from his books, and a condensed version of *Johnson over Jordan*. Ralph Richardson, now the right age, created a spell that lifted the heart.

In 1954 Priestley wrote an article called 'Jung and the Writer' for the *Times Literary Supplement*. With Jung on his mind he went to see Bernard Shaw's *Don Juan in Hell* in New York, directed by Charles Laughton. This gave him the idea for *Dragon's Mouth*, a 'platform drama' for four characters, who would represent Jung's four functions of sensation, emotion, intellect and intuition. He planned to write it with Jacquetta in their first collaboration. She was with him in New York, and began to work on it immediately. Priestley was to write two of the characters – Matthew, the tough businessman, and his woman secretary, and Jacquetta would write Matthew's wife (my part, Nina) and Michael's part Stuart, the academic. As Nina I had the privilege of speaking a really wonderful piece about a seagull – one of the best bits of writing I have ever had to play.

The story was about these four characters on Matthew's yacht moored in an inlet called Dragon's Mouth, in the West Indies. A plague has broken out among the crew, and one of them has died and two more are stricken. A doctor, called to see the sick crewmen, has also taken blood samples from the four making the cruise, and they know that if anyone has been affected it means certain death.

There was no scenery, only a rope to represent the side of the yacht, and four high stools. The whole performance took place on the yacht's deck, where the characters discuss their lives, their approach to life, and their views about themselves. At first they are satisfied with the way each of them lives, but after the doctor's visit the mood changes. The characters forget all pretence, and all posturing, exposing themselves quite truthfully. Nina speaks for both Jung and Jacquetta, and Jacquetta wrote about herself profoundly. As the critic Kenneth Tynan admitted, the play has several flights of the best rhetorical prose he had heard on stage.

Dragon's Mouth went on an extraordinary and tiring tour of one-night stands, but was always a pleasure to perform. The tour was a reasonable success, and the play then came into the Winter Garden Theatre (now demolished), where it ran for seven weeks, to mixed criticism but to (for the most part) extremely appreciative audiences.

Among Priestley's other plays, *Eden End* (1934), *Laburnum Grove* (1933), and *The Linden Tree* (1947), and much later *A Severed Head* (1963) had considerable success. *A Severed Head*, which was a collaboration with Iris Murdoch, ran for nearly two years at the Criterion Theatre. It was an adaptation of Iris's own novel of the same name which she had tried to adapt herself, but failed. When she took it to Priestley he said, 'This won't do, Duckie.' He had known Iris since her early novel writing days and had regarded her as a major new talent. They had become friends immediately, 'I adored him at once,' she said.

They worked together happily, and Iris felt that Jack had taught her a great deal – though the dialogue in *A Severed Head* is very different from that in any other of his straight plays, being tart and sophisticated, with no magic around. It was almost a year before they found a cast and a theatre, but the play was a triumph. Since this was Priestley's last major involvement in plays, he was able to leave the theatre with guns blazing.

SIX

JANE, INFIDELITY AND JACQUETTA

Talking to Tom Priestley (born in 1932) about his mother Jane, he said he remembered her as having brown hair and brown eyes, that he believed she would like to have been a boy, that she was a caring mother, very clever and good at languages, excellent with finances, taking charge of the now very good money Priestley was making, and she made each of the houses they rented or owned beautiful. Her gift for decoration was such that she even decorated the Duchess Theatre in London, which it was rumoured Priestley had contemplated buying at one time. She asked for binoculars as payment. Decorating was her creativity – home life for the children was comfortable but rigidly formal, with the nanny the centre of their universe, and apart from Sunday lunches they only visited their parents for an hour in the evenings.

She helped Priestley with his work, for years discussing all his writing with him, and he depended a good deal on her criticisms. She introduced him to French literature; she also to everyone else's relief had a gift for making her husband laugh when he was in one of his bad moods. She was fairly often ill, some of her ailments probably a psychosomatic reaction to his infidelities, but her pregnancy with Tom was so difficult that for two years afterwards they wintered in Arizona where the dry climate helped her considerably. She brought up all the children: Barbara and Sylvia (Pat Tempest's children); Angela Wyndham Lewis, who had to change her Christian name from Barbara to Angela when Barbara Priestley joined the family; Mary, Priestley's illegitimate child with Jane, who attributed her later mental troubles to the shock she had when she discovered she was illegitimate, and Tom and Rachel, born after Priestley and Jane were married. Tom described Rachel as the most independent of the children.

In spite of such a full domestic life Priestley embarked on a series of affairs. He had always preferred women's company to that of men, saying he found them much more interesting, and seemed to consider infidelity a perfectly normal way of conducting a marriage. It is ironic that Jane had divorced her first husband for unfaithfulness.

Some time in early 1931 Priestley met Peggy Ashcroft, perhaps when he was writing a non-fiction book called *I'll Tell You Everything* (1932) in the Cotswolds with Gerald Bullett, and she was acting in *Hassan* in nearby Oxford. He fell instantly in love with her, and was totally obsessed, following her everywhere, declaring his passion. Peggy was already well known as a brilliant young actress, who had married the actor (later the distinguished publisher) Rupert Hart-Davis two years before when she was aged twenty-three. In June 1931, on a brief visit to England from Broadway, New York, Priestley told a devastated Jane that he loved Peggy and wanted to marry her. Jane wrote despairingly to Edward Davison about it, saying that she had believed her marriage to be intact and that she loved her husband as much as she always had, in spite of one or two quarrels about his mistresses.

Peggy always maintained that although immensely flattered that such a famous author admired her so extravagantly, she was never in love with him, and that they never had a real affair. Priestley refused to give her up, appearing like a jack-in-the-box at his home, either telling Jane he was in love with Peggy and wanted to marry her, or that he had finished with her. A distraught Jane first took all the children to Cornwall where she and Priestley had a reconciliation which resulted in the birth of Tom, then she said she would leave Priestley or not, as he wished. Until just before Christmas 1931 this see-saw situation continued, driving Jane nearly out of her mind. At last Priestley said that he had truly left Peggy for good, although it is more likely that she left him, because she had now become involved with Theodore Komisajevsky, the theatre director, again much older than she – Priestley was thirty-six, Komisajevsky fifty-three. She created a scandal by living with Komisajevsky in 1932, and married him the following year. The marriage was short-lived.

Priestley's children were made very upset by the whole affair – but he himself managed to continue writing a prodigious amount which, as always, was the inner core of his being. As well as *I'll Tell You Everything*, he was arranging for *The Good Companions* to be produced in his own dramatisation. He also wrote a new light comedy called 'The Roundabout' for Peggy and Diana Wynyard (which he ultimately abandoned), started on a new novel *Wonder Hero* (1933) and wrote a book column for the *Evening News*.

When Priestley heard Jane was pregnant, he wanted her to have an abortion. Jane disagreed, and won the day. In the end both were delighted with their son.

The second major entanglement which could have ruined the Priestley marriage occurred during the Second World War. Mary Hope Allen (later Mary Merrington) was an extremely pretty and intelligent BBC producer. Priestley met her in a lift in Manchester, followed her out when she left it, and told her he had seen her often nearly twenty years before attending every London first night with well-known people like Herbert

Farjeon. He later invited her to dinner at the
Midland Hotel.

They soon fell in love. Although Priestley was
recording his 'Postscripts' to huge audiences, and
had become even more nationally and
internationally famous, Mary was delighted by his
modesty, and she told his biographer Vincent Brome
that he once put his arm round her and said 'This is
custom made, you fit just over my heart.'[1]

The affair lasted five years, during most of which
Jane appeared unaware, and the rest of the family
remained in total ignorance. Priestley wrote Mary a
flood of passionate letters, but never stopped
writing very affectionately to Jane. As usual his
work continued unabated and he wrote four plays
and seven books during their relationship.

Although Priestley said he preferred women to
men and disliked 'boys' talk' he had many men
friends – Hugh Walpole being probably the greatest.
They wrote extremely affectionate letters to each
other, but although Walpole was homosexual there
was no sort of liaison between them. Priestley's
friendship with Edward Davison, which began in
Cambridge, lasted until the latter's death in 1970,

and Ralph Richardson, Norman Collins, H.G. Wells, Robert Lynd, J.M. Barrie, Gareth Lloyd Evans (and his wife Barbara) and Charles Laughton were also very good friends. There were a great many more. He had a gift for friendship.

But a time bomb was ticking for Jane. In 1947 Priestley met the great love of his life, Jacquetta Hawkes. Soon after the war was over the United Nations had set up a number of large organisations, one of which was UNESCO, the United Nations Educational Scientific and Cultural Organisation, and an inaugural six weeks' meeting was to be held in Mexico at the end of the year. Sir John Maude in the Ministry of Education was the head of the department responsible, and chose Priestley as a delegate to represent literature and the arts in general. Jacquetta Hawkes, his secretary, was very against the idea. As Sir John was adamant, Jacquetta had to write to Priestley to ask him if he would accept. She signed her letters J.J. Hawkes and Priestley assumed she was a man.

In July they met at a reception for senior delegates in Paris where Jacquetta and another woman, Helen de Mouliplied, had been assigned as his two special assistants. Helen cancelled the trip on the grounds of ill health, and Priestley set sail for Mexico with Jacquetta as his only assistant. She was an exceedingly bad sailor and spent most of the journey confined in her cabin. In Mexico City she fell ill again, this time with gastroenteritis, in the insalubrious hotel where they were billeted, and Priestley visited her in her room with brandy in a medicine bottle. Like many other women Jacquetta was seduced by his voice, and basked in the way she felt cared for. When she recovered they wined and dined and took long walks together, feeling as she described it 'created anew', and also feeling that she had been 'filled with the recognition of the sweet tragedy of mortal love'. When the trip was over they agreed that as both had families (Jacquetta was married to the archaeologist Christopher Hawkes and had a son Nicholas) there was to be no future for them. However, Jack immediately started writing her love letters, once again continuing to write in his usual affectionate manner to Jane.

For the next six years he lived his usual complicated double life, as always writing his books, plays and articles. He met Jacquetta as often as he could in borrowed flats, in country woods and once even in a provincial theatre box. Jane seemed not to know about the affair for some time but was going through a very difficult period with their daughter Mary, which culminated in Mary's complete nervous breakdown. She was diagnosed as a manic depressive, but in time recovered and sublimated the experience by turning her musical gift as a professional violinist into becoming a music therapist. Priestley's work at this time included an opera libretto, *The Olympians* (1949), *An Inspector Calls* and *The Linden Tree* (1948), which were running in London but needed attention. He was also writing *The Golden Fleece* (1948), *Home is Tomorrow* (1949) and *The High Toby* (1948), a puppet play for children, as well as pieces for newspapers and magazines. He also became a member of the Royal Commission on the Press, and chairman of the British Theatre Conference, the London Philharmonic Advisory Council, and the National Theatre Institute in Prague.

Jessie Jacquetta Hopkins was the daughter of one of the most famous scientists of the day – Sir

Frederick Gowland Hopkins OM, who won a Nobel Prize, discovered vitamins, and led the field in biochemistry. Jacquetta's mother, Jessie Anne Stevens, an orphan, was a probationer nurse at the Royal Free Hospital in London when they met and married within months of their meeting. Jacquetta, the youngest of their children, was born in 1910. Her mother was kind, beautiful, loyal and ran a comfortable home, and the children were taken to art galleries and museums from an early age. Jacquetta became a self-reliant and precocious child and, like her mother, a beautiful woman, dark-haired and slender with a fascinating secret smile and an air of cool detachment. At Newnham College, Cambridge, she took a first-class honours degree in archaeology and anthropology and won a travelling scholarship, on which she went to the caves at Mount Carmel in Palestine, and supervised the recovery of a Neanderthal skeleton.

After marrying Christopher Hawkes, whose mother hated her, Jacquetta left London in 1940 with their son Nicholas to escape the air raids and stay in Dorset with a friend called Betty Pinney, with whom she fell in love – a love which was neither enthusiastically reciprocated nor consummated. She returned to her parents' home in Cambridge for weekends, spending the weeks with Christopher in their house in Hampstead. In 1943 she fell in love with a married poet and critic, Walter Turner, aged sixty (she was now thirty-three), and they had a passionate affair, though neither thought of leaving their spouses. In 1946 Turner died from a brain haemorrhage, leaving Jacquetta in despair. Eight months later she met Priestley.

After he met Jacquetta, Priestley was never unfaithful again, and their marriage was an idyllic partnership until he died, except for one rift between them about her sapphic affair. In fact, for everyone concerned, there was happiness – Jane, Priestley's second wife, was very happy with Dr Bannerman, as was Christopher Hawkes with his second wife.

SEVEN

POSTSCRIPTS – FAMILY–TRAVELLING

On Sunday 3 September 1939, the day war broke out, Jane drove Priestley to London to deliver to the BBC the first instalment of the script of his novel *Let the People Sing* (1939). It was to be broadcast in serial form. Shortly afterwards he suggested that he should do some propaganda broadcasting for them and they allotted a slot for him immediately after the nine o'clock news. He began, too, a series of Ministry of Information articles for the *News Chronicle*, but he found the Ministry badly organised with too many civil servants and not enough journalists. He felt that those in power in the country had not grasped the fact that this particular war depended for success on people's morale almost more than anything else, as the previous war had finished not long ago, and most people had no stomach for a new one. Consequently, he broadcast the 'Postscripts', nineteen of them, between 5 June and 20 October 1940.

They were an instant success – radio then was the most important method of communication, and Priestley became a consummate broadcaster. Winston Churchill, the Prime Minister of the Coalition Government, broadcast magnificent speeches in some of the finest oratory ever heard, and the two men, Priestley down to earth, homely, uplifting, funny and sometimes literary, and Churchill grand, exciting, comforting and somehow enormously dependable, did indeed keep up the national morale. Gradually, though, a body of people began to suspect Priestley of socialist propaganda, and after the first series ended, A.P. Herbert, Clemence Dane and Emlyn Williams were brought in to succeed him. All failed, so Priestley was given a second series on 26 January 1941. This time the right-wing press were gunning for him, although in March *Picture Post* did a large and important feature on him, very much on his side. Finally, however, to his fury he was taken off the air. Incidentally, during the 'Postscripts' he had booked in at the Langham Hotel opposite the BBC in Portland Place because the bombing was becoming so heavy and constant that Jane took the children to Wales. One night he decided to remain in the BBC cellars instead. The Langham was hit, and his room completely destroyed.

His other writing fell sharply during the war, though most writers did not come near the body of work he achieved. He wrote four plays, including *They Came to a City* (1943), and started *An Inspector Calls*, finalised two 'war' novels, and completed four official commissions on war topics including *British Women Go to War* (1943). He also broadcast regularly to the USA and the Dominions.

His home background more or less disintegrated. The house, 3 The Grove, in Highgate, London, to which the family had moved in 1931, was sold. Billingham Manor, the beautiful old house they had bought in the Isle of Wight, was commandeered by the Black Watch, and the Priestleys' possessions looted and stolen, including Jane's clothes and a painting by Augustus John. Priestley moved between the Langham Hotel and a friend's flat, finally renting in 1943 Flat B3 and B4, in Albany, Piccadilly, the apartment fictionally inhabited by John Worthing in Oscar Wilde's *The Importance of Being Earnest*.

Jane took on a series of war jobs, keeping Tom and Rachel with her wherever she went. At the beginning of the war all the children except Angela, who was at the Oxford Playhouse, were at boarding school, and then Barbara studied architecture and had a wartime job at the Ministry of Town and Country Planning. Sylvia went to the Slade School in London to study art, then joined the WRNS, and Mary left school at sixteen and went to the Royal College of Music.

The year 1945 saw the publication of a fairly indifferent novel, *Three Men in New Suits*, and a pamphlet about what should happen after the war called 'Letter to a Returning Soldier', but also to universal surprise Priestley decided to stand for Cambridge University as an independent candidate in the general election. He only came in a poor third — after which the Priestleys tried to settle down again together. They kept the Albany flats, and looked at Billingham, which had been given back to them, but found it in a terrible state. In September 1945 they went together to Russia, where Jane's gift for languages was a great help. The visit was a personal success, but Russia had been so devastated that they were appalled by the starvation and the conditions after the bombing. In January 1946 Priestley had a bad attack of pneumonia. Billingham was very expensive to restore and although their former domestic help had returned, it was difficult to keep up. Worst of all, the relationship between the Priestleys had badly deteriorated. They had lived independent lives for too long. Billingham was sold and they found a large house with wonderful views called Brook Hill.

In 1949 Priestley's play *A Summer Day's Dream* was given fifty performances at the St Martin's Theatre. It was also adapted for television with Sir John Gielgud as the star. By the 1950s Priestley was having difficulty with his writing. New writers – John Osborne with *Look Back in Anger* and Samuel Beckett with *Waiting for Godot* – were changing the face of drama. Plays such as Priestley's *Bright Shadow*

(1959) and *Treasure on Pelican* (1952) seemed out of date. *Take the Fool Away* (1956) was not highly regarded, and the novel *Festival at Farbridge* (1951), although quite popular with the public, and the Book Society Choice for May 1951, was not well reviewed. Ralph Richardson disliked 'Golden Door' (1951), which never went into production. Meanwhile Jacquetta's book *A Land* (1957) was acclaimed. In 1952 *The White Countess*, the Priestleys' second dramatic collaboration, failed miserably. Immediately afterwards they went to Japan.

In 1952 Jacquetta and Christopher Hawkes were divorced, as were the Priestleys. In 1953 Jack and Jacquetta married at the Caxton Hall Registry Office in London. In 1956, things literary began to improve. *Mr Kettle and Mrs Moon* opened in London and fared quite well, and then in 1957 *Journey Down a Rainbow* had excellent notices. More importantly, as a regular contributor to Kingsley Martin's *New Statesman* and given the idea by Martin's assistant John Freeman, Priestley wrote the piece which is generally believed to have launched the Campaign for Nuclear Disarmament (CND). Since Freeman was not anti-bomb himself, Priestley obtained all the articles in favour of the bomb from the *New Statesman* library and these he carefully and powerfully demolished. His article 'Britain and the Nuclear Bomb' created a sensation almost as great as his 'Postscripts'. In response to the thousands of letters received by the *New Statesman*, Kingsley Martin called a meeting at his flat to which Sir Stephen King-Hall, George Kennan (who in 1957 had given the Reith lectures on 'Russia, the Atom and the West'), and P.M.S. Blackett were invited. The meeting decided to launch a major national campaign – there was already a small one headed by Bertrand Russell called the 'Campaign Against Nuclear Weapons'. Russell and Peggy Duff, the leader of another small Hampstead group, joined CND. Peggy Duff suggested that Canon John Collins, who with his wife Diana was well known for his anti-apartheid views on South Africa, might be asked to let his home in the cathedral precinct of St Paul's be used as a meeting place. Priestley had doubts about the Collinses and arranged to meet them at his flat in

Albany. In the event Canon Collins had to cry off, but Diana went, as did Laurens van der Post's wife Ingaret. Diana and Priestley instantly became friends. So later did Canon Collins. The friendship lasted for the rest of their lives and in 1961 Priestley dedicated his thriller *Saturn Over the Water* to them.

At first CND, launched at Central Hall, Westminster, was enthusiastically supported by both Priestley and Jacquetta. Priestley made speeches all over the country, and in 1958 wrote a play for television called *Doomsday for Dyson*. He also organised a fundraising event at the Festival Hall, but he never joined the famous marches, unlike Jacquetta and Canon Collins, Jacquetta often wearing a rather large Russian military hat. Jacquetta also set up a women's group of well-known writers and scientists who lobbied Downing Street and the Geneva Conference, and in 1962 the United Nations in New York and the White House. Priestley eventually resigned from CND. All his life he had disliked being involved with large organisations, and when Bertrand Russell left, he left too.

In 1960 he published *Literature and Western Man*, an enormous book covering 700 authors from the fifteenth century and the Renaissance to the present day. Personal rather than academic, it took him eighteen months to write. In Britain it was a great success, but it was not popular in America.

In 1959 the Priestleys sold Brook Hill and bought Kissing Tree House near Stratford-upon-Avon, where they lived until Jack died. Jacquetta ran the house rather formally, though she was a warm and welcoming hostess with what Priestley called her 'magnificent grin', but not all of his many friends interested her, and they were quietly dropped. They both loved the house and Priestley started painting – mostly landscapes in gouache. He found he painted well and the pastime became a passion.

Two other passions were his love of music and of pictures, about both of which he knew a great deal. In *Particular Pleasures* (1975) he wrote about both in a highly personal way, about Breughel the Elder, Watteau, Hogarth, Constable, Turner, Corot, Cézanne, Gauguin, Sickert, Bonnard and Paul Nash being some of his favourite painters, and about

Rossini, Berlioz, Schumann, Bruckner, Brahms, Dvorák and Elgar being some of his favourite musicians.

In 1962, too, he wrote *Margin Released*, a brilliant collection of memoirs, and in 1964 the amusing novel, *Sir Michael and Sir George*. These were followed in 1965 by one of his finest novels, *Lost Empires*, the 'Lost Empires' being the old Empire music halls. Its hero, Richard Herncastle, is a clever, jobless, young artist in the idyllic pre-1914 years in Yorkshire, which so haunted Priestley all his life. Richard is taken on by his uncle, a magician and illusionist, and they tour the Lost Empires. It is my own favourite of his novels. Priestley's favourites were the two novels, *Out of Town* and *London End* (both 1968), which combined make up 'The Image Men'. They are funny, but for me the humour is overstretched.

In 1961 he wrote *The Shapes of Sleep* and between 1964 and 1969 *Man and Time* (1964), *The Moments* (1966), a novella *The Thirty First of June* (1966), *Trumpets Over the Sea* (1968), *The Prince of Pleasure* (1969), *The World of Charles Dickens* (1969 — Dickens was a great hero of Priestley's) and collections of his own previous works, *The World of J.B. Priestley* (1967), *All England Listened* (the 'Postscripts', 1968) and *Essays of Five Decades* (1969). In 1969 Bradford University gave him the honorary degree of Doctor of Letters.

EIGHT

THE 1970S AND 1980S

M any of Priestley's friends died in 1970, including Edward Davison in the spring, but his writing went on. Two books from this decade are particularly fascinating, *The Edwardians* (1970), beautifully illustrated with photographs, and *Victorian Heyday* (1972). He also travelled a great deal, going on a tiring trip to New Zealand which he enjoyed, in spite of recovering from a minor operation at the time – he had always enjoyed travelling ever since his long-ago days in the wool trade. Formerly his trips to America for both work and pleasure gave him a love–hate relationship with the country. The Priestleys had an extraordinary and influential time there, with Jacquetta visiting the native reservations of the Navaho and Zuni Indians, and Jack lecturing in Texas, so that they could write a book comparing their joint experiences (*Journey Down a Rainbow*, 1955). Jacquetta fell in love with the Indians and their lifestyle, especially the Zuni, but in her part of the book she wrote a chapter on Los Alamos, which she also visited with Priestley, which was where the first successful explosion of the atomic bomb had taken place. Both were powerfully affected by the implications of what it stood for, and in a way it was responsible for their later involvement in CND.

In 1974 Priestley returned briefly to the theatre, overseeing a musical of *The Good Companions* with music by André Previn, lyrics by Johnny Mercer and starring Sir John Mills, Judi Dench and Christopher Gable (the dancer). Priestley was delighted with it. It opened in Chichester but only had six months in London. In 1973 he was given the Freedom of the City in his home town of Bradford, and was offered several honours including a knighthood, Companion of Honour, and a life peerage. All these he refused. He did, though, accept the OM in 1977 to the delight of all his friends. Old age was now slowing him down physically, and insomnia, which had plagued him earlier, returned. He mused on time and death. In

Instead of Trees (1977) he wrote an essay on the subject, saying that he did not accept the case for extinction.

Towards the end of his life he seldom left Kissing Tree House and his adored Jacquetta, and eventually he gave up writing. Then the depression he had always tried to keep at bay came back. He loved seeing his family and friends, but now in the 1980s his health deteriorated. He had a strange attack when Barbara and Gareth Lloyd Evans were staying with him, sliding suddenly to the ground holding two drinks, neither of which he spilled! He explained it by saying he was 'bored'. He became deaf, which he hated, and had short-term memory loss. In February 1984 he had several gastric attacks which necessitated an operation and intensive care, and when Barbara and Sylvia, his daughters, came to see him to make arrangements for a birthday lunch for him on 13 September, he caught pneumonia and never really recovered. Barbara, Sylvia, Jacquetta and the loyal and wonderful Miss Pudduck all took turns to sit by him so that he was never on his own.

On the night of 13–14 August 1984 he died peacefully. Jacquetta gently kissed him and said,

'Goodbye, my love' – and in the garden owls hooted.

Priestley was cremated privately, and had a memorial service in Westminster Abbey at which Dame Peggy Ashcroft read the essay 'Whatever happened to Falstaff?' His ashes are in the graveyard of the tiny church in the little village of Hubberholme, in his beloved Yorkshire Dales.

In her book, *A Quest for Love* (1980), Jacquetta had written in the last paragraph, 'Nowadays Jack keeps the Malacca stick I gave him long ago, and the huge beret we bought in Bordeaux lying in readiness for an afternoon walk. I have only to look at these two dear objects for my heart to turn over.'[1]

N O T E S

CHAPTER ONE

1. Judith Cook, *Priestley*, p. 4.
2. *New Statesman*, 29 July 1966.
3. Priestley, *Margin Released*, p. 78.
4. Priestley, *Bright Day*, p. 16.
5. Ibid., pp. 16–17.

CHAPTER TWO

1. *Margin Released*, p. 82.
2. Ibid., p. 93.
3. Ibid., pp. 99–100.
4. Ibid., pp. 153–4.
5. Cook, *Priestley*, p. 85.

CHAPTER THREE

1. Cook, *Priestley*, p. 85.
2. Cook, *Priestley*, p. 95.

CHAPTER FOUR

1. Priestley, *Particular Pleasures*, p. 175.
2. Priestley, *Delight*, pp. 11–12.

Notes

Chapter Five

1.   Cook, *Priestley*, pp. 297–8.

Chapter Six

1.   Vincent Brome, *J.B. Priestley*, p. 264 .

Chapter Eight

1.   Jacquetta Hawkes, *A Quest for Love*.

BIBLIOGRAPHY

Atkins, John Alfred, *J.B. Priestley: The Last of the Sages*, London, J. Calder, Riverrun Press, 1981

Braine, John, *J.B. Priestley*, London, Weidenfeld & Nicolson, 1978

Brome, Vincent, *J.B. Priestley*, London, Hamish Hamilton, 1988

Collins, D., *Time and the Priestleys*, Stroud, Alan Sutton, 1994

Cook, Judith, *J.B. Priestley*, London, Bloomsbury Publishing, 1997

Cooper, S., *Portrait of an Author*, London, Heinemann, 1970

Evans, G. Lloyd, *J.B. Priestley, Dramatist*, London, Heinemann, 1974

Hawkes, Jacquetta, *A Quest for Love*, London, Chatto & Windus, 1980

Priestley, J.B., *Delight*, London, Heinemann, 1949

———, *Margin Released*, London, Heinemann, 1962

———, *Particular Pleasures*, London, Heinemann, 1975

P R I E S T L E Y ' S   W O R K S

FICTION

1927   *Adam in Moonshine*

1928   *Benighted*

1929   *Farthing Hall* (with Hugh Walpole)

1929   *The Good Companions*

1930   *The Town Mayor of Miraucourt*

1930   *Angel Pavement*

1932   *Faraway*

1933   *Wonder Hero*

1936   *They Walk in the City*

1937   *The Doomsday Men*

1939   *Let the People Sing*

1942   *Blackout in Gretley*

1943   *Daylight on Saturday*

1945   *Three Men in New Suits*

1946   *Bright Day*

1954   *The Magicians*

1961   *Saturn Over the Water*

1961   *Salt is Leaving*

1965   *Lost Empires*

1968   The Image Men: vol. 1 *Out of Town*, vol. 2 *London End*

1971   *Snoggle*

1975   *The Carfitt Crisis*

NON-FICTION

1918   *The Chapman of Rhymes*

1922   *Brief Diversions*

1922   *Papers from Lilliput*

1923   *I for One*

1924   *Figures in Modern Literature*

1926   *George Meredith*

1926   *Essays of Today and Yesterday*

1927   *Open House* (essays)

1927   *Thomas Love Peacock*

1927   *The English Novel*

1928   *Apes and Angels*

1929   *English Humour*

1929   *The Balconinny and Other Essays*

1932   *Self-Selected Essays*

1932   *I'll Tell You Everything — J.B. Priestley and Gerald Bullett*

1933   *English Journey*

1936   *Charles Dickens*

1937   *Midnight on the Desert, A Chapter of Autobiography*

1939   *Rain Upon Godshill, A Further Chapter of Autobiography*

1940   *Postscripts*

1941   *Out of the People*

1942   *Britain at War*

1943   *British Women Go to War*

1944   *Manpower*

1946   *Russian Journey*

1946   *The Secret Dream*

1947   *Arts Under Socialism*

1949   *Delight* (essays)

1951   *The Priestley Companion*

1955   *Journey Down a Rainbow*

1956   *The Writer in a Changing Society*

1956   *All About Ourselves and Other Essays*

1957   *The Art of the Dramatist*

1957   *Thoughts in the Wilderness* (essays)

1960   *Literature and Western Man*

1961   *Charles Dickens – A Pictorial Biography*

1962   *Margin Released*

1964   *Man and Time*

1966   *The Moments*

1967   *The World of J.B. Priestley*

1969   *Essays of Five Decades*

1969   *The Prince of Pleasure*

1969   *Charles Dickens and His World*

1970   *The Edwardians*

1972   *Victoria's Heyday*

1972   *Over the Long High Wall* (essays)

1973   *The English*

1974   *A Visit to New Zealand*

1974   *Outcries and Asides* (essays)

1975   *Particular Pleasures* (essays)

1976   *English Humour*

1977   *Instead of the Trees* (essays)

PRIESTLEY'S PLAYS IN ORDER OF PERFORMANCE

1931   *The Good Companions* (adaptation)

1932   *Dangerous Corner*

1933   *Laburnam Grove*

1933   *The Roundabout*

1934   *Eden End*

1935   *Duet in Floodlight*

1936   *Bees on the Boat Deck*

1936   *Spring Tide*

1937   *I Have Been Here Before*

1937   *Time and the Conways*

1937   *People at Sea*

1938   *Mystery at Greenfingers*

1938   *Music at Night*

1938   *When We Are Married*

1939   *Johnson Over Jordan*

1940   *The Long Mirror*

1942   *Good Night Children*

1943   *They Came to a City*

1943   *Desert Highway*

1944   *How Are They At Home?*

1946   *An Inspector Calls*

1947   *Ever Since Paradise*

1947   *The Linden Tree*

1947   *The Rose & Crown*

1948   *The Golden Fleece*

1948   *Home is Tomorrow*

1948   *The High Toby*

1949   *Summer Day's Dream*

1950   *Bright Shadow*

1952   *Dragon's Mouth* (with Jacquetta Hawkes)

1952   *Treasure on Pelican*

1953   *Private Rooms*

1953   *Mother's Day*

1954   *A Glass of Bitter*

1955   *Mr Kettle and Mrs Moon*

1956   *Take the Food Away*

1958   *The Glass Cage*

1963   *A Severed Head* (with Iris Murdoch)

1963   *The Pavilion of Masks*

POCKET BIOGRAPHIES

Beethoven
Anne Pimlott Baker

Mao Zedong
Delia Davin

Scott of the Antarctic
Michael De-la-Noy

Alexander the Great
E.E. Rice

Sigmund Freud
Stephen Wilson

Marilyn Monroe
Sheridan Morley and
Ruth Leon

Rasputin
Harold Shukman

Jane Austen
Helen Lefroy

Ellen Terry
Moira Shearer

David Livingstone
C.S. Nicholls

Abraham Lincoln
H.G. Pitt

**Marie and Pierre
Curie**
John Senior

Margot Fonteyn
Alastair Macaulay

Enid Blyton
George Greenfield

Winston Churchill
Robert Blake

George IV
Michael De-la-Noy

For a copy of our complete list or details of other Sutton titles, please contact Sarah Flight at Sutton Publishing Limited, Phoenix Mill, Thrupp, Stroud, Gloucestershire, GL5 2BU

POCKET BIOGRAPHIES

Christopher Wren
James Chambers

Cleopatra
E.E. Rice

Che Guevara
Andrew Sinclair

John Ruskin
Francis O'Gorman

W.G. Grace
Donald Trelford

Joseph Stalin
Harold Shukman

The Brontës
Kathryn White

Juan and Eva Perón
Clive Foss

Lawrence of Arabia
Jeremy Wilson

Queen Victoria
Elizabeth Longford

Christopher Columbus
Peter Riviere

Anthony Trollope
Graham Handley

Martin Luther King
Harry Harmer

Byron
Catherine Peters

Genghis Khan
James Chambers

Fidel Castro
Clive Foss

James Dean
William Hall

J.B. Priestley
Dulcie Gray